TRADING AND INVEST

The ultimate guide on how to Trade for a Living with Time-tested Strategies and Techniques.

William Grey

This document is geared towards providing exact and reliable information in regards to the topic and issue covered. The publication is sold with the idea that the publisher is not required to render accounting, officially permitted, or otherwise, qualified services. If advice is necessary, legal or professional, a practiced individual in the profession should be ordered.

- From a Declaration of Principles which was accepted and approved equally by a Committee of the American Bar Association and a Committee of Publishers and Associations.

The information herein is offered for informational purposes solely and is universal as such. The presentation of the information is without a contract or any type of guarantee assurance.

Introduction

A great many amateurs take a shot at the market gambling club every year, except most leave a little less fortunate and significantly more intelligent, having never arrived at their maximum capacity. Most of the individuals who fall flat make them think in like manner: They haven't dominated the essential abilities expected to shift the chances in support of themselves. Notwithstanding, on the off chance that one sets aside satisfactory effort to learn them, it's feasible to be en route to expand one's chances of achievement.

World markets pull in theoretical capital like moths to fire; a great many people toss cash at protections without understanding why costs move sequentially. All things being equal, they pursue hot tips, make double wagers, and sit under masters, allowing them to settle on purchase and sell choices that have neither rhyme nor reason. An excellent way is to figure out how to trade the markets with expertise and authority.

Start with a self-assessment that investigates your relationship with cash. Do you see life as a battle, with an arduous exertion needed to acquire every dollar? Do you accept that personal attraction will pull in market abundance to you similarly in other life pursuits? All the more forebodingly, have you lost cash consistently through different exercises and expect the financial markets will treat you all the more generous?

Whatever your conviction framework, the market will probably build up that interior view again through benefits and misfortunes. Challenging work and appeal both help financial achievement, yet washouts in different backgrounds will probably transform into failures in the exchanging game. Try not to freeze if this seems like you. Take the self-improvement course and find out about the connection between cash and self-esteem.

When you get your head on straight, you can figure out how to trade and begin with these five important advances.

Step 1: Open a Trading Account, Buy and Sell

Sorry on the off chance that it appears we're expressing the self-evident; however, you won't ever know! (Recall the individual who did everything to set up his new PC—but to connect it?) Find a decent online stock specialist and open a stock investment fund. Regardless of whether you have a personal account, it is anything but a poorly conceived notion to keep an expert exchanging account independently. Come out as comfortable with the account interface and exploit the free exchanging devices and examination offered solely to customers. Various agents offer a virtual exchange. A few destinations, including Investopedia, additionally offer online specialist audits to help you track down the correct agent.

Picking the correct money market fund can appear to be a troublesome cycle; however, it doesn't need to be. By choosing what kind of account you need and afterwards contrasting a few online stock dealers, you ought to have the option to pick the one that best addresses your issues.

Here's your bit by bit direct for opening a trade account:

1. Determine the type of brokerage account you need

What are your investment targets? Suppose you need to contribute for a stormy day or a specific moderately near term objective and don't need your cash restricted until you resign. In that case, a conventional money market fund is the best approach. These accounts don't have charge benefits - you may need to pay the charge on investment benefits and profits - yet you are allowed to pull out your cash at whatever point you'd like. Hence, a customary or standard money market fund is regularly alluded to as an available investment fund.

On the off chance that you pick a conventional investment fund, your merchant will probably inquire whether you need a money account or an edge account. If you decide to apply for edge advantages, this essentially implies that you can get cash to purchase stocks, with the stocks in your portfolio filling in as security. You'll pay revenue on the acquired cash, and there are some intrinsic dangers implied with contributing on edge that you ought to know about.

Then again, if you will likely set aside cash for retirement, an IRA is the smartest choice. Conventional IRAs can get you to charge allowances when you add to them; however, you will not have the option to utilize your cash until you're 59-1/2. Commitments to Roth IRAs don't give you a tax cut when you make them; however, qualified Roth IRA withdrawals will be tax-exempt. Also, you can pull out Roth IRA commitments (yet not your investment benefits) at whatever point you need. At last, in case you're independently employed, there are some great alternatives for you, like a SIMPLE IRA, SEP-IRA, or individual 401(k). You can peruse a more careful manual to help you pick the best IRA too.

It's likewise essential that numerous individuals open various investment funds - like an available account and an IRA, to keep their cash in isolated crates.

2. Compare the costs and incentives

Nowadays, essentially the entirety of the significant rebate specialists offer sans commission exchanging. They may likewise offer you a markdown to compensate you for specific activities, for example, moving a vast investment account from another agent.

It's imperative to survey each online financier company's complete evaluating plan, especially on the off chance that you plan on exchanging something besides stocks (alternatives, shared assets, ETFs, bonds, and so forth), as these regularly accompany their expenses. For instance, numerous merchants charge a commission in the scope of $0.50 to $0.75 per choices contract, so regardless of whether the representative doesn't charge a base commission, choices exchanging will not by and large be free.

At last, numerous dealers offer motivating forces to draw in business, and you don't should be a tycoon to exploit them. I'm not saying that a decent motivating force without help from anyone else should influence your choice; however, it's very a piece of the riddle worth contemplating.

Valuing isn't all that matters - particularly for new financial backers. Any remaining things being equivalent, it's ideal for tracking down the most minimal cost, yet here are a couple of different things you need to consider when picking an intermediary:

Admittance to explore: Many dealers give their stock appraisals, just as admittance to outsider exploration from firms like Standard and Poors and Morningstar.

Unfamiliar exchanging: Some specialists offer the capacity to change over cash in your account into unfamiliar monetary forms to trade on global stock trades. If this is essential to you, ensure the representative you pick permits this.

Fragmentary offers: This can be particularly critical to new financial backers, as you don't really should have the option to manage the cost of an exclusive offer to begin putting resources into your number one stocks.

Exchanging stages: The different businesses offer a wide assortment of exchanging programming and versatile applications, and numerous permit individuals to try out their foundation before opening an account. For instance, Fidelity offers a demo adaptation of its Active Trader Pro stage for imminent customers to test-drive. Likewise, read a few surveys of specialists' versatile applications if having the option to get to your account in a hurry is imperative to you.

Comfort: Some financiers have huge neighbourhood office workplaces you can visit for up close and personal investment direction, while others don't. For instance, Merrill Edge clients can get one-on-one counsel and direction over 2,000 Bank of America areas. Additionally, businesses worked by banks offer clients the capacity to interface their financier and financial records, moving cash between the accounts progressively - and may offer a type of "relationship markdown" for doing as such. Thus, it's likewise a smart thought to check if your bank has an online business, regardless of whether it's not referenced here.

Different highlights: This is anything but a comprehensive rundown, so before you pick an agent, make sure to invest some energy on its site investigating what it offers.

4. Choosing a Proprietary Trading Firm

At the point when I left Swift Trade Securities, it was friendly. I had been offered a salaried position at that branch of Swift on my re-visitation of Toronto, which I would later come to learn was an unimaginably rare proposal to be given to previous traders at any non-bank proprietary trading firm.

Regardless of all the harmful exposure related to Swift Trade—or its author's resulting substances—in its dealings with Canadian regulators, or the impression that many may have about its trading strategies based on simple verbal, Swift Trade Securities was undeniably a superb place for a trainee to start in the trading industry, especially in the era previously and during the early implementation of Reg NMS and the Hybrid NYSE market. What's more, it is fair to say that my particular reasons for leaving the company were all together for practical and personal reasons. Not the slightest bit reflected how I was treated and trained at the company. Leaving it was probably one of the most egotistical decisions I at any point made in my career inside the protections trading industry—which says a considerable amount in a business that should be driven by primal dynamics of personal gain and cutthroat competition.

You've gathered your information about various firms' expenses, charges and the conveniences they offer. For each brokerage, you ought to gauge the upsides and downsides of your investment goals and figure out which specialist is ideal for you.

At the point when I left Swift Trade Securities, it was friendly. I had been offered a salaried position at that branch of Swift on my re-visitation of Toronto, which I would later come to learn was an amazingly rare proposal to be given to previous traders at any non-bank proprietary trading firm.

Regardless of all the harmful exposure related to Swift Trade—or its originator's resulting substances—in its dealings with Canadian regulators, or the impression that many may have about its trading strategies based on simple informal, Swift Trade Securities was undeniably a brilliant place for a trainee to start in the trading industry, especially in the era previously and during the early implementation of Reg NMS and the Hybrid NYSE market. In addition, it is fair to say that my particular reasons for leaving the company were entirely for practical and personal reasons and not the slightest bit reflected how I was treated and trained at the company. Leaving it was probably one of the most egotistical decisions I at any point made in my career inside the protections trading industry—which says a considerable amount in a business that should be driven by primal dynamics of personal gain and cutthroat competition.

You've gathered your information about various firms' expenses, charges and the conveniences they offer. For each brokerage, you ought to gauge the advantages and disadvantages as they pertain to your investment targets and figure out which specialist is appropriate for you.

The way you decide to trade will rely upon your situation. You can change your trading type when you're going; however, it takes time and money, so it's ideal for hitting the nail on the head the first time.

Sole Trader

Many small organizations track down this as the most practical solution. It's undoubtedly the least complex way to maintain a one-person business. It's more straightforward and easier to set up than a local company; also, you won't have anyone else to answer to.

All the benefits from the business will be yours, yet you'll also be liable for any business obligations. In case you're independently employed, you need to enlist with HM Revenue and Customs.

Partnership

At least two independently employed individuals are cooperating, sharing the benefits and misfortunes. You ought to know that each partner is personally responsible for the misfortunes regardless of whether someone else caused them. If you're going into a partnership, it's a smart thought to draw up a composed agreement between partners to secure individual interests.

Restricted Liability Partnerships (LLP)

This is organized and taxed like a partnership; however, it offers restricted liability for business obligations. At least two individuals or local companies share in the expenses, benefits and responsibilities of the company.LLPs should be enlisted at Companies House, and annual accounts should be filed. Members can restrict their responsibilities, yet there should be at least two designated individuals who have additional responsibilities placed upon them by law.

Restricted Company

This is generally more complicated and costly to set up than a partnership or sole trader business. To become a limited company, you should create and send a Memorandum and Articles of Associations, along with a registration charge and reports, to Companies House. These reports layout the accompanying:

- Company name – there are a few restrictions on words you can have in your name, and it can't be the same or similar to one already enlisted.
- Enlisted address – this isn't always where you operate the business from. Frequently it will be the street number of a Director or the workplace of the company's accountant or specialist.
- The company will keep this broad, for example, 'commercial retailer' as your activities will be restricted to this.
- Details of Company Directors
- How the company will be run
- Privileges of the company's shareholders.

Companies House can assist you with finishing structures and Company names; however, not with the content of any documentation. Annual accounts should be submitted to Companies House, and for an expense, anyone can take a gander at them. Limiting your liability is the main advantage of setting up a restricted company. When in doubt, you will only lose the amount put resources into the company should anything go wrong? The company can also continue after the original Directors leave, giving the company a longer life expectancy than a partnership or sole trader.

5. Fill out the new account application

You can apply to open another account online, and this is generally a speedy and painless cycle with online representatives. You'll require some recognizing information, for example, your Social Security number and driver's permit. You may have to sign additional structures if you're mentioning margin advantages or the ability to trade options. The dealer should gather information about your total assets, work status, investable assets, and investment goals.

6. Fund the account

Your new online broker will probably give you a few options to move money into your account, including:

Electronic funds transfer (EFT): Transferring funds from a linked checking or savings account is a convenient way to fund the account. In most cases, the funds will post to the account on the following business day.

Wire transfer: The quickest way to fund your account. Since a wire transfer is a direct bank-to-bank transfer of money, it often takes place within minutes.

Checks: Acceptable forms of check deposits and fund availability vary between brokers.

Asset transfer: If you're rolling over a 401(k) or transferring existing investments from another broker, that's an acceptable funding method.

Stock certificates: Yes, these still exist. If you have a paper stock certificate, it can be deposited via mail into an online brokerage account.

As a final note, when funding your new account, be sure to keep your broker's minimums in mind. Many have different minimums for taxable accounts and retirement accounts, and they also may have different minimum requirements for margin accounts.

7. Start researching investments

Congratulations on taking the initiative and opening a brokerage account -- your future self will thank you for taking this vital step on the road toward financial security.

Now comes the fun part: investing in stocks. Before diving in, it's a good idea to spend some time learning the basics of how to responsibly choose stocks, bonds, and funds, as well as how to create a well-diversified portfolio.

Buy and sell trade

To buy stocks, you need the assistance of a stockbroker since you cannot usually call up a company and ask to buy their store on your own. There are two basic categories of representatives to look over for unpracticed financial backers: a full-administration specialist or an online/rebate agent.

Full-Service Brokers

Full-administration merchants are what a great many people visualize when they think about contributing—fashionable, cordial money managers sitting in an office chatting with customers. These are the traditional stockbrokers who will take an opportunity to become more acquainted with you personally and financially. They will take a gander at factors like marital status, way of life, personality, hazard tolerance, age (time horizon), pay, assets, obligations, and more. By becoming more acquainted with as much about you as they can, these full-administration agents can then assist you with fostering a long-term financial plan.

Not exclusively can these intermediaries assist you with your investment needs, yet they can also give assistance estate planning, tax advice, retirement planning, planning, and any other sort of financial advice, subsequently the expression "full-administration." They can assist you with managing your economic necessities now and long into the future and are for financial backers who want everything in one package. As far as charges, full-administration representatives are more costly than rebate facilitates, yet the value in having a professional investment advisor close by can be definitely worth the additional expenses. Accounts can be set up with as little as $1,000. The vast majority, especially novices, would fall into this category as far as the kind of merchant they require.

How do buyers and sellers affect the markets?

At any given time, one gathering will, in general, exceed the other, and that's one of the reasons the cost of a market fluctuates. At the point when the buyers exceed the sellers, demand for the market rises. Therefore, the cost of the asset climbs. When it's the alternate way round, supply increases and direction for the support starts to drop – and the price falls.

What do 'buy' and 'sell' mean in trading?

At the point when you open a 'buy' position, you are essentially buying an asset from the market. And when you close your work, you 'sell' it back to the market. Buyers – also known as bulls – accept an asset's value is probably going to rise. Sellers – or bears – generally think its value is set to fall.

At the point when you open a position with a representative or trading supplier, you'll be given two costs. You open a' long' work on the off chance that you want to trade at the buy value, which is somewhat above the market value. If you're going to deal at the selling cost – somewhat beneath the market cost – you open a 'short position. The distinction between the buy and sell cost is known as the 'spread', which the supplier takes to facilitate the position.

What is a long position?

A long position in traditional trading is the point at which you buy an asset in the expectation its cost will rise so that you can sell it later for a benefit. This is also alluded to as going long or buying.

Making a long trade doesn't necessarily mean buying a physical asset. Derivatives like CFDs and fates contracts offer you the chance to take a long position on a market without possessing hidden support. You are essentially speculating that the cost of the asset will rise.

What is a short position?

A short position in trading is a strategy used to take advantage of markets falling in cost. When you make a quick trade, you are selling an acquired asset to expect that its price will go down, and you can repurchase it later for a benefit. It is also known as short-selling, shorting or going short.

Short-selling works by acquiring the fundamental asset from a trading dealer and then immediately selling it at the current market cost. Shorting is something contrary to going long – where you will benefit if the price goes up.

Again, suppose you want to trade bitcoin against the US dollar (bitcoin/USD). The current market cost is 3919, and you decide to take a short position and sell five contracts (each equivalent to 1 BTC) to open a place at this cost.

If you were correct, and the value of bitcoin fell against the US dollar, your trade would benefit. Suppose that the new market cost is 3874. You could close your position and take your benefit by buying five contacts to complete your place at the buy cost of 3879, which is marginally higher than the market cost because of the spread. Because the market has moved 40 focuses in your favour, the benefit on your trade would be calculated as follows: 5 x 40 = $200. If the market moved against you by 40, you would have made a misfortune, calculated as 5 x - 40 = - $200.

How to go long and short on markets

If you want to take a long or short position on a market, you can open a CFD trading account. CFD trading is the buying (going long) and selling (going shy) of contracts at the distinction in cost of an asset, between the opening and shutting of your position.

CFDs are derivative items because they enable you to speculate on financial markets like shares, forex, records, and wares without taking responsibility for hidden assets. The two techniques use leverage, which means you only have to set up a small margin (store) to gain openness to the total value of the trade. This can magnify your potential benefit, yet additionally your possible misfortune.

How buyers and sellers affect the market

Buyers and sellers affect market interest – and like this, the cost – of an asset. At any given time, one gathering will, in general, exceed the other, and that's the primary reason the price of a market fluctuates. At the point when the buyers exceed the sellers, demand for the market rises. Accordingly, the cost of the asset rises. When it's the opposite way around, supply increases and direction for the asset starts to drop – and the price falls. The way market interest affect markets are regularly alluded to as volatility.

A buyer's market is when buyers have the advantage over sellers. They can negotiate a premium buying cost for an asset because supply is far more than demand. A seller's market is a restricted stockpile of an investment and a flood of buyers. In this case, the seller has the advantage.

When to buy a Stock

How to Buy Stocks

Buying stocks isn't as complicated as it appears, yet you'll have to do some research — and learn the dialect — before you make your first investment.

To buy stocks, you'll initially require a brokerage account, which you can set up in about 15 minutes. At that point, once you've added money to the store, you can follow the means underneath to discover, choose and put resources into individual companies.

It may appear to be confusing from the beginning, yet buying stocks is beautifully straightforward. Here are five stages to help you buy your first stock:

1. Select an online stockbroker

The easiest way to buy stocks is through an online stockbroker. After opening and subsidizing your account, you can buy stocks through the intermediary's site surprisingly fast. Different options incorporate utilizing a full-administration stockbroker or buying stock straightforwardly from the company.

Opening an online brokerage account is as easy as setting up a bank account: You complete an account application, give evidence of identification and pick whether you want to support the version via mailing a check or transferring reserves electronically.

2. Research the stocks you want to buy

Once you've set up and financed your brokerage account, it's an ideal opportunity to plunge into the matter of picking stocks. A decent place to start is by researching companies you already know from your encounters as a consumer.

Don't let the storm of data and real-time market gyrations overpower you as you conduct your research. Keep the goal basic: You're searching for companies to turn into a part proprietor.

Warren Buffett famously said, "Buy into a company because you want to possess it, not because you want the stock to go up." He's done quite well for himself by observing that standard.

Once you've recognized these companies, it's an ideal opportunity to do a little research. Start with the company's annual report — specifically management's annual letter to shareholders. The letter will give you a general narrative of what's happening with the business and provide context to the numbers in the report.

After that, most of the information and analytical apparatuses you need to evaluate the business will be available on your specialist's site, like SEC filings, conference call transcripts, quarterly earnings updates, and late news. Most online specialists also give tutorials on the best way to utilize their apparatuses and even introductory seminars on the best way to pick stocks.

3. Decide the number of shares to buy

You should feel no strain to buy a certain number of shares or fill your whole portfolio with stock all at once. Consider starting small — really small — by purchasing simply a solitary share to discover what it resembles to claim individual stocks and whether you have the grit to ride through the difficult times with minimal rest misfortune. You can add to your position after some time as you master the shareholder swagger.

New stock financial backers may also want to consider fractional shares, a relatively new contribution from online agents that allows you to buy a portion of a stock rather than the total stake. What that means is you can get into expensive stores — companies like Google and Amazon that are known for their four-figure share costs — with a lot smaller investment. SoFi Active Investing, Robinhood and Charles Schwab are among the dealers that offer fractional shares. (SoFi Active Investing and Robinhood are NerdWallet advertising partners.)

Many brokerages offer an instrument that converts dollar amounts to shares, as well. This can be useful if you have a set amount you'd prefer to contribute — say, $500 — and want to know the number of shares that amount could buy.

4. Pick your stock request type

There are many more fancy trading moves and complex request types. Don't trouble at this moment — or maybe ever. Financial backers have assembled fruitful careers buying stocks exclusively with two request types: market requests and cutoff orders.

Market orders

With a market request, you're indicating that you'll buy or sell the stock at best available current market cost. Because a market request puts no value parameters on the trade, your request will be executed immediately and filled, except if you're attempting to buy a million shares and attempt a takeover overthrow.

Don't be amazed if the value you pay — or get, in case you're selling — isn't the exact value you were cited only seconds prior. Offer and ask costs constantly fluctuate for the day. That's the reason a market request is best utilized when buying stocks that don't encounter wide value swings — large, steady blue-chip stocks rather than smaller, more volatile companies.

Great to know:

A market request is best for buy-and-hold financial backers, for whom slight contrasts in cost are less important than guaranteeing that the trade is entirely executed.

On the off chance that you place a market request trade "after hours," when the markets have shut for the afternoon, your request will be placed at the overall cost when the exchanges next open for trading.

Check your intermediary's trade execution disclaimer. Some minimal expense agents group, all client trade solicitations, execute all at once at the overall cost, either at the finish of the trading day or a particular time or day of the week.

Breaking point orders

A breaking point request gives you more control over the cost at which your trade is executed. If XYZ stock is trading at $100 a share and you think a $95 per-share price is more following how you value the company, your cutoff request advises your merchant to hold tight and execute your request only when the asking value drops to that level. On the selling side, a cutoff request suggests your merchant part with the shares once the bid ascends to the level you set.

Breaking point orders are a decent apparatus for financial backers buying and selling smaller company stocks, which will, in general, experience more extensive spreads, contingent upon financial backer activity. They're also helpful in contributing during short stock market volatility or when the stock cost is a higher priority than request satisfaction.

You can place additional conditions on a limit request to control how long the request will remain open. An "all or none" (AON) request will be executed only when all the shares you wish to trade are available at your value limit. A "useful for day" (GFD) request will terminate at the finish of the trading day, regardless of whether the request has not been filled. A "great till canceled" (GTC) request remains in play until the client reassesses or requests lapses; that's anywhere from 60 to 120 days or more.

Great to know:

While a cutoff request guarantees the cost you'll get if the request is executed, there's no guarantee that the request will be filled, partially or even at all. Cutoff orders are placed on a first-come, first-served basis, and only aftermarket orders are filled, and only if the stock stays inside your set parameters long enough for the specialist to execute the trade.

Breaking point requests can cost financial backers more in commissions than market orders. A cutoff request that can't be executed in full at once or during a solitary trading day may continue to be filled over ensuing days, with transaction costs charged each day a trade is made. If the stock never reaches your breaking point request level when it terminates, the business won't be executed.

5. Streamline your stock portfolio

We trust your first stock purchase marks the start of a lifelong excursion of effective contributing. In any case, if things turn troublesome, recall that each financial backer — even Warren Buffett — goes through difficult times. The way to outpacing the competition in the long term is to keep your point of view and concentrate on what you can control. Market gyrations aren't among them. Be that as it may, there are a couple of things in your control.

Once you're familiar with the stock purchasing measure, take an opportunity to delve into different areas of the investment world. How might mutual assets play a part in your investment story? In addition to a brokerage account, have you set up a retirement account, like an IRA? Opening a brokerage account and buying stocks is a significant initial step, yet it's the start of your investment venture.

Understanding Stock Options Trading

Trading stocks can measure up to betting in a gambling club: You're wagering against the house, so if every one of the clients have a mind blowing line of karma, they could all success.

Trading choices is more similar to wagering on ponies at the course: Each individual wagers against the wide range of various individuals there. The track essentially takes a little cut for giving the offices. So trading alternatives, such as wagering at the pony track, is a lose-lose situation. The alternative purchaser's benefit is the choice vender's misfortune and the other way around.

One significant contrast among stocks and alternatives is that stocks give you a little piece of proprietorship in an organization, while choices are simply gets that give you the option to purchase or sell the stock at a particular cost by a particular date.

It's critical to recollect that there are consistently different sides to each choice exchange: a purchaser and a dealer. As such, for each alternative bought, there's consistently another person selling it.

Sorts of Options

The two sorts of choices are calls and puts. At the point when you purchase a call choice, you have the right, yet not the commitment, to buy a stock at a set cost, called the strike value, any time before the alternative terminates. At the point when you purchase a put choice, you have the right, however not the commitment, to sell a stock at the strike value any time before the lapse date.

At the point when people sell choices, they successfully make a security that didn't exist previously. This is known as composing a choice, and it clarifies one of the fundamental wellsprings of choices since neither the related organization nor the choices trade gives the alternatives.

At the point when you compose a call, you might be committed to sell shares at the strike value any time before the termination date. At the point when you compose a put, you might be committed to purchase shares at the strike value any time before termination.

There are additionally two essential styles of choices: American and European. An American-style alternative can be practiced whenever between the date of procurement and the termination date. An European-style choice must be practiced on the termination date. Most trade traded choices are American style, and all stock choices are American style. Many record alternatives are European style.

Alternative Pricing

The cost of an alternative is known as the premium. The purchaser of a choice can't lose more than the underlying premium paid for the agreement, regardless of what befalls the basic security. So the danger to the purchaser is never more than the sum paid for the choice. The benefit potential, then again, is hypothetically limitless.

As a trade-off for the premium got from the purchaser, the merchant of an alternative expects the danger of conveying (if a call choice) or taking conveyance (if a put choice) of the portions of the stock. Except if that alternative is covered by another choice or a situation in the hidden stock, the dealer's misfortune can be open-finished, which means the merchant can lose substantially more than the first premium got.

If it's not too much trouble, note that alternatives are not accessible at simply any cost. Stock choices are for the most part traded with strike costs in time periods or $1, yet can likewise be in timespans and $5 for more extravagant stocks. Likewise, just strike costs inside a sensible reach around the current stock cost are by and large traded. Far in-or out-of-the-cash alternatives probably won't be accessible.

Alternative Profitability

At the point when the strike cost of a call choice is over the current cost of the stock, the call isn't productive or out-of-the-cash. All in all, an investor won't accepting a stock at a greater cost (the strike) than the current market cost of the stock. At the point when the call choice strike cost is underneath the stock's value, it's considered in-the-cash since the investor can purchase the stock at a lower cost than in the current market.

Put choices are the specific inverse. They're considered out-of-the-cash when the strike cost is beneath the stock cost since an investor wouldn't sell the stock at a lower value (the strike) than in the market. Put alternatives are in-the-cash when the strike cost is over the stock cost since investors can sell the stock at the higher (strike) cost than the market cost of the stock.

Lapse Dates

All stock choices terminate on a specific date, called the lapse date. For ordinary recorded alternatives, this can be as long as nine months from the date the choices are first recorded for trading. Longer-term alternative agreements, called long haul value expectation protections (LEAPS), are likewise accessible on numerous stocks. These can have termination dates as long as three years from the posting date.

Choices lapse at market close on Friday, except if it falls on a market occasion, in which case termination is moved back one work day. Month to month choices terminate on the third Friday of the lapse month, while week after week choices lapse on every one of different Fridays in a month.

In contrast to portions of stock, which have a two-day settlement period, alternatives settle the following day.5In request to choose the lapse date, you need to exercise or trade the choice before the day's over on Friday.

Trading choices are altogether different from trading stocks since alternatives have unmistakable qualities from stocks. Investors need to set aside the effort to comprehend the phrasing and ideas associated with choices before trading them.

Choices are monetary subordinates, implying that they get their worth from the fundamental security or stock. Alternatives give the purchaser the right, yet not the commitment, to purchase or sell the hidden stock at a pre-decided cost.

Understanding Stock Options Trading

Trading stocks can measure up to betting in a gambling club: You're wagering against the house, so if every one of the clients has a mind-blowing line of karma, they could all succeed.

Trading choices are more similar to wagering on ponies at the course: Each wager against the wide range of various individuals there. The track essentially takes a happens cut for giving the offices. So trading alternatives, such as wagering at the pony track, is a lose-lose situation. The alternative purchaser's benefit is the choice vendor's misfortune and the other way around.

One significant contrast between stocks and alternatives is that stores give you a little piece of proprietorship in an organization. At the same time, choices get give you the option to purchase or sell the stock at a particular cost by a specific date.

It's critical to recollect that there are consistently different sides to each choice exchange: a purchaser and a dealer. As such, for each alternative bought, there's always another person selling it.

Sorts of Options

The two sorts of choices are calls and puts. At the point when you purchase a call choice, you have the right, yet not the commitment, to buy a stock at a set cost, called the strike value, any time before the alternative terminates. At the point when you purchase a put choice, you have the right, however not the commitment, to sell a stock at the strike value any time before the lapse date.

At the point when people sell choices, they successfully make security that didn't exist previously. This is known as composing a choice, and it clarifies one of the fundamental wellsprings of options since neither the related organization nor the choices trade gives the alternatives.

At the point when you compose a call, you might be committed to selling shares at the strike value any time before the termination date. At the point when you compose a put, you might be committed to purchase shares at the strike value any time before termination.

There are additionally two basic styles of choices: American and European. An American-style alternative can be practiced whenever between the date of procurement and the termination date. A European-style choice must be practiced on the termination date. Most trades traded choices are American style, and all stock choices are American style. Many record alternatives are European style.

Alternative Pricing

The cost of an alternative is known as the premium. The purchaser of choice can't lose more than the underlying premium paid for the agreement, regardless of basic security. So the danger to the purchaser is never more than the sum paid for the choice. The benefit potential, then again, is hypothetically limitless.

As a trade-off for the premium got from the purchaser, the merchant of an alternative expects the danger of conveying (if a call choice) or taking conveyance (if a put choice) of the portions of the stock. Except if that alternative is covered by another choice or a situation in the hidden stock, the dealer's misfortune can be open-finished, which means the merchant can lose substantially more than the first premium got.

If it's not too much trouble, note that alternatives are not accessible at simply any cost. For the most part, stock choices are traded with strike costs in periods or $1, yet can likewise be in timespans and $5 for more extravagant stocks. Again, strike costs inside a sensible reach around the current stock cost are primarily traded. Far in-or out-of-the-cash alternatives probably won't be accessible.

Alternative Profitability

When the strike cost of a call choice is over the stock's current price, the call isn't productive or out-of-the-cash. All in all, an investor won't accept a store at a more significant cost (the strike) than the current market cost of the stock. When the call choice strike cost is underneath the stock's value, it's considered in-the-cash since the investor can purchase the stock at a lower price than in the current market.

Put choices are the specific inverse. They're considered out-of-the-cash when the strike cost is beneath the stock cost since an investor wouldn't sell the stock at a lower value (the strike) than in the market. Put alternatives are in-the-cash when the strike cost is over the stock cost since investors can sell the stock at a higher (strike) cost than the market cost of the stock.

Chapter 2: Learn and Practice Trading

Financial articles, stock market books, site tutorials, and so on, there's a wealth of information out there and a lot of it economical to tap. It's essential not to zero in too narrowly on one single aspect of the trading game. Instead, study everything market-wise, including ideas and concepts you don't feel are particularly relevant at this time. Trading launches an excursion that regularly ends up at a destination not anticipated at the starting line. Your broad and detailed market background will prove to be useful again and again, regardless of whether you think you know exactly where you're going at this moment.

Here are five must-read books for each new trader:

- Stock Market Wizards by Jack D. Schwager
- Trading for a Living by Dr Alexander Elder
- Technical Analysis of the Financial Markets by John Murphy
- Winning on Wall Street by Martin Zweig
- The Nature of Risk by Justin Mamus

Start to follow the market each day in your spare time. Rise and shine early and read about, for the time being, value action on foreign markets. (U.S. traders didn't have to monitor global markets years and years ago, yet that's all changed because of the rapid development of electronic trading and derivative instruments that connect value, forex and bond markets around the world.)

News locales, for example, Yahoo Finance, Google Finance, and CBS MoneyWatch, fill in as a great asset for new financial backers. For more sophisticated coverage, you need to look no farther than The Wall Street Journal and Bloomberg.

Trading is the act of buying and selling a financial instrument around the same time or even on various occasions throughout a day. Taking advantage of small value moves can be a lucrative game—on the off chance that it is played effectively. However, it very well may be a dangerous game for amateurs or anyone who doesn't adhere to a thoroughly examined strategy.

Not all merchants are appropriate for the high volume of trades made by day traders, in any case. In any case, a few merchants are planned in light of the day trader. You can look at our rundown of the best specialists for day trading to see which dealers best accommodate the individuals who might want to day trade.

The online merchants on our rundown, Fidelity and Interactive Brokers, have professional or advanced versions of their platforms that feature real-time streaming statements, advanced charting instruments, and the ability to enter and adjust complex orders one after another.

Underneath, we'll take a glance at some general day trading standards and then proceed onward to deciding when to buy and sell, common day trading strategies, basic charts and patterns, and how to restrict misfortunes.

1. Information Is Power
In addition to information on basic trading methodology, day traders need to keep up on the latest stock market news and occasions that affect stocks—the Fed's loan fee plans, the economic standpoint, and so forth.

So get your work done. Make a list of things to get of stocks you'd prefer to trade and keep yourself educated about the chose companies and general markets. Scan business news and visit reliable financial sites.

2. Set Aside Funds
Assess how much capital you're willing to hazard on each trade. Many fruitful day traders assume under 1% to 2% of their account per trade. On the off

chance that you have a $40,000 trading account and will hazard 0.5% of your capital on each trade, your maximum misfortune per trade is $200 (0.5% * $40,000).

Put away an excessive amount of assets you can trade with, and you're prepared to lose. Keep in mind, it may or may not happen.

3. Set Aside Time, Too

Day trading requires your time. That's the reason it's called day trading. You'll have to surrender the more significant part of your day. Please don't consider it on the off chance that you have restricted extra time.

The cycle requires a trader to track the markets and spot openings, which can arise at any time during trading hours. Rushing is critical.

4. Start Small

As a novice, centre around a maximum of one to two stocks during a session. Tracking and discovering openings is more accessible with only a couple of stores. As of late, it has gotten increasingly common to have the option to trade fractional shares so that you can determine exact, smaller dollar amounts you wish to contribute.

That means if Apple shares are trading at $250 and you only want to buy $50 worth, many agents will currently allow you to purchase one-fifth of a claim.

5. Avoid Penny Stocks

You're probably searching at deals and low costs; however, stay away from penny stocks. These stocks are frequently illiquid, and the chances of hitting the jackpot are regularly bleak.

Many stocks trading under $5 a share become de-recorded from major stock exchanges and are only tradable over-the-counter (OTC). Except if you see a real chance and have done your research, stay clear of these.

6. Time Those Trades

Many orders placed by financial backers and traders start to execute as soon as the markets open in the first part of the day, which contributes to value volatility. A seasoned player may have the option to perceive patterns and pick appropriately to make benefits. However, it could be better for amateurs to read the market without making any moves for the initial 15 to 20 minutes.

The centre hours are usually less volatile, and then development starts to get again toward the end chime. Even though the busy times offer freedoms, it's safer for amateurs to avoid them from the beginning.

7. Cut Losses With Limit Orders

Decide what kind of orders you'll use to enter and leave trades. Will you utilize market requests or cutoff orders? When you place a market request, it's executed at the best cost available at the time—accordingly, no value guarantee.

A breaking point request, meanwhile, guarantees the cost yet not the execution. Breaking point orders help you trade with more precision, wherein you set your price (not unrealistic yet executable) for buying and selling. More sophisticated and experienced day traders may utilize the utilization of options strategies to support their positions as well.

8. Be Realistic About Profits

A strategy doesn't have to win all an opportunity to be profitable. Many traders only win half to 60% of their trades. Be that as it may, they make more on their victors than they lose on their failures. Ensure the danger on each trade is restricted to a particular percentage of the account and that section and leave techniques are characterized and recorded.

9. Stay Cool

There are times when the stock markets test your nerves. As a day trader, you need to learn to keep ravenousness, expectation, and fear at bay. Decisions ought to be represented by rationale and not emotion.

10. Stick to the Plan

Effective traders have to move fast; however, they don't have to think fast. Why? Because they've fostered a trading strategy in advance, along with the order to adhere to that strategy. It is essential to follow your formula intently rather than attempt to chase benefits. Don't allow your emotions to trick you and abandon your strategy. There's a mantra among day traders: "Plan your trade and trade your plan."

Before we go into a portion of the intricate details of day trading, we should take a gander at a part of the reasons why day trading can be so troublesome.

What Makes Day Trading Difficult?

Day trading takes a great deal of practice and ability, and several factors can make the interaction challenging.

To begin with, realize that you're going toward professionals whose careers rotate around trading. These individuals have access to the best innovation and connections in the business, so regardless of whether they fail, they're set up to prevail eventually. If you get on board with the bandwagon, it means more benefits for them.

Uncle Sam will also want a cut of your benefits, regardless of how thin. Recall that you'll have to pay taxes on any short gains—or any investments you hold for one year or less—at the marginal rate. The one caveat is that your misfortunes will counterbalance any gains.

As an individual financial backer, you may be prone to emotional and psychological biases. Professional traders can usually remove these of their trading strategies; however, when it's your capital included, it will, in general, be an alternate story.

Day Trading Charts and Patterns

To help decide the ideal second to buy a stock (or whatever asset you're trading), many traders use:

- Candlestick patterns, including inundating candles and dojis
- Technical analysis, including pattern lines and triangles
- Volume—increasing or decreasing.

There are many candlestick arrangements a day trader can search for to discover a section point. Whenever utilized appropriately, the Doji reversal pattern (featured in yellow in the chart beneath) is one of the most reliable ones.

Typically, search for a pattern like this with several confirmations:

- In the first place, search for a volume spike, which will show you whether traders support the cost at this level. Note: this can be either on the Doji candle or on the candles immediately following it.
- Second, search for earlier help at this value level—for example, the earlier low of day (LOD) or high of day (HOD).
- Finally, take a gander at the Level 2 situation, which will show all the open requests and request sizes.

If you follow these three stages, you can decide if the dog will probably deliver an actual turnaround and take a position if the conditions are favourable.

Traditional analysis of chart patterns also gives benefit targets to exits. For example, the tallness of a triangle at the most significant part is added to the breakout point of the triangle (for a potential gain breakout), giving a cost at which to take benefits.

to Limit Losses When Day Trading Step by step instructions

A stop-misfortune request is intended to restrict misfortunes on a position in a security. A stop misfortune can be placed under an extraordinary failure for long positions or short positions above a new high. It can also be based on volatility.

For example, assuming a stock cost is moving about $0.05 a moment, you may place a prevent misfortune $0.15 away from your entrance to give the value some space to fluctuate before it moves in your anticipated direction.

Characterize precisely how you'll control the danger of the trades. For instance, on account of a triangle pattern, a stop misfortune can be placed $0.02 under a new swing low if buying a breakout, or $0.02 beneath the way. (The $0.02 is arbitrary; the fact of the matter is to be explicit.)

One strategy is to set two stop misfortunes:

- A physical stop-misfortune request placed at a certain value level that suits your danger tolerance. Essentially, this is the most money you can stand to lose.
- A mental stop-misfortune set at where your entrance criteria are violated. This means if the trade makes an unforeseen turn, you'll immediately leave your position.

Any way you decide to leave your trades, the leave criteria should be sufficiently explicit to be testable and repeatable. Also, it's essential to set a maximum misfortune each day you can afford to withstand—both financially and mentally. At whatever point you hit this point, take the remainder of the day off. Adhere to your Plan and your borders. After all, tomorrow is another (trading) day.

Once you've characterized how you enter trades and where you'll place a stop misfortune, you can assess whether the potential strategy fits inside your danger limit. If the approach uncovered many hazards, you need to alter the strategy somehow or another to diminish the danger.

If the strategy is inside your danger limit, testing starts. Manually pass through historical charts to discover your entrances, noticing whether your stop misfortune or target would have been hit. Paper trade in this way for at least 50 to 100 trades, seeing whether the strategy was profitable and if it lives up to your desires.

On the off chance that it does, continue to trade the strategy in a demo account in real-time. If it's profitable throughout two months or more in a simulated environment, continue with day trading the strategy with natural capital. If the strategy isn't good, start over.

Finally, remember that if trading on margin—which means you're getting your investment assets from a brokerage firm (and bear as a primary concern that margin prerequisites for day trading are high)— you're far more vulnerable to sharp value developments. Margin assists with amplifying the trading results of benefits, however, of misfortunes if a trade conflicts with you. Consequently, utilizing stop misfortunes is crucial when day trading on margin.

Since you know a portion of the intricate details of day trading, how about we take a brief gander at a part of the critical strategies new day traders can utilize.

Basic Day Trading Strategies

Once you've mastered a portion of the procedures, fostered your very own trading styles, and figured out what your ultimate objectives are, you can utilize a progression of strategies to help you as you continued looking for benefits.

Here are some popular strategies you can utilize. Although a portion of these has been mentioned above, they merit going into again:

- **Following the pattern:** Anyone who follows the pattern will buy when costs are rising or short sell when they drop. This is done on the assumption that costs that have been rising or falling steadily will continue to do as such.
- **Contrarian contributing:** This strategy assumes the ascent in costs will opposite and drop. The contrarian buys throughout the fall or short-sells during the rise, expressing the expectation that the pattern will change.
- **Scalping:** This is a style where a speculator misuses small value gaps created by the bid-ask spread. This procedure includes typically entering and leaving a position rapidly—inside the space of minutes or even seconds.
- **Trading the News:** Investors utilizing this strategy will buy when uplifting news is announced or short sell when there's wrong information. This can lead to greater volatility, which can lead to higher benefits or misfortunes.

Day trading is hard to master. It requires time, expertise, and control. Many of the individuals who attempt it fail, yet the methods and rules portrayed above can assist you with creating a profitable strategy. With enough practice and consistent performance evaluation, you can significantly improve your chances of beating the events.

Learn to Analyze

Study the basics of technical analysis and see value charts—thousands of them—in all periods. You may think fundamental analysis offers a superior path to benefits because it tracks development bends and income streams. Yet, traders live and kick the bucket by value action that wanders sharply from hidden fundamentals. Try not to quit reading company spreadsheets because they offer a trading edge over the individuals who overlook them. Notwithstanding, they won't assist you with enduring your first year as a trader.

Your involvement in charts and technical analysis currently carries you into the magical realm of value prediction. Theoretically, protections can only go sequential, encouraging a long-side trade or a short sale. In reality, costs can do many different things, including cleaving sideways for quite a long time at a time or whipsawing savagely in the two directions, shaking out buyers and sellers.

The time horizon turns out to be critical at this point. Financial markets pound out patterns and trading ranges with fractal properties that generate autonomous value developments at the present, intermediate-term, and long-term intervals. This means a security or file can carve out a long-term upswing, intermediate downtrend, and a short trading range, all at the same time. Rather than complicate prediction, most trading openings will unfurl through interactions between these time intervals.

Buying the plunge offers a classic example, with traders bouncing into a strong upswing when it sells off in a lower period. The ideal way to examine this three-dimensional playing field is to take a gander at each security in three-time spans, starting with hour-long, daily and week after week charts.

TECHNICAL ANALYSIS CHARTS: TALKING POINTS

Technical analysis of charts aims to distinguish patterns and market drifts using varying types of specialized chart types and other chart functions.

Deciphering charts can be intimidating for amateur traders, so understanding fundamental technical analysis is essential. This article reveals popular sorts of technical analysis charts utilized in forex trading, illustrating the foundations and employments of these chart types.

What number of TYPES OF CHARTS ARE THERE?

There are three main kinds of technical analysis charts: candlestick, bar, and line charts. They are all created utilizing the same value data; however, they unexpectedly display the data. Therefore, they include various kinds of technical analysis to help traders make educated decisions across forex, stocks, records and products markets. While there are several unique kinds of charts, this article covers only the main three because these three are the most generally followed.

The three charts introduced underneath have been chosen as they are universal across most trading platforms.

TOP 3 TYPES OF TECHNICAL ANALYSIS CHARTS FOR TRADING

Line Charts

- Best for trading: Stocks
- Trading experience: Beginner
- Technical analysis procedure: Holistic market outline which eliminates moving data
- Advantages: Supports trading without the impact of emotions

A line chart typically displays shutting costs, and that's it. Each end cost is connected to the past shutting cost to make a continuous line that is easy to follow.

This kind of chart is frequently utilized for television, newspapers and many web articles because it is essential and easy to process. It gives less information than candlestick or bar charts, yet it is better for survey at a glance for an oversimplified market see.

Another advantage of the line chart is that it can assist in managing the emotions of trading by choosing a neutral tone, similar to the blue chart portrayed above. This is because the line chart eliminates 'rough' developments in various shadings as found in the bar and candlestick charts.

Master tip: Due to the line chart illustrating only shut costs, more experienced traders will consider a line chart to map out the daily shutting costs or situations when the analyst wants to assess the sub-waves without the clamour.

Bar (HLOC) Charts

- Best for trading: Forex, stocks, files and items
- Trading experience: Intermediate
- Technical analysis procedure: Use value data (HLOC) to distinguish patterns, support/resistance, and passage focuses
- Advantages: Provides the trader with more detail which assists with distinguishing key levels and top to bottom data

A bar chart displays the high, low, open and shutting (HLOC) costs for each period designated for the bar. The vertical line is created by the high and low cost for the bar. The dash to one side of the bar was the opening cost, and the energy to the correct signals the end cost.

Having the option to distinguish whether a bar quits for the day or down (red) indicates to the trader the market slant (bullish/bearish) for that period.

The similarities between this chart type and a candlestick chart are noticeable when seen one next to the other; however, a bar chart is better for a cleaner market to see. By eliminating the bolded shading from the chart, traders can see market patterns from an uncomplicated standpoint.

Candlestick Charts

- Best for trading: Forex, stocks, lists and wares
- Trading experience: Intermediate

- Technical analysis procedure: Equivalent to the bar chart strategy (dependant on trader inclination)
- Advantages: Candlesticks are easier on the eye for traders instead of bar charts because of the whole nature of the candlestick

A candlestick chart displays the high, low, open and shutting (HLOC) costs for each period designated for the candle. The "body" of each candlestick addresses the opening and closing costs, while the candle "wicks" displays the high and low prices for each period.

The shade of each candle relies upon the applied settings; however, most charting packages will utilize green and red as the default tones. The green candles mirror cost a shut higher than where it opened (regularly called a bullish candle), and each candle that is red means the cost shut lower than where it opened (frequently called a bearish candle).

The candlestick chart is by a wide margin the most popular kind of chart utilized in technical forex analysis as it furnishes the trader with more information while remaining easy to see at a glance.

Instructions to Analyze TECHNICAL CHARTS

Charting strategies in technical analysis will vary contingent upon the strategy and market being traded. It is essential to be familiar and comfortable with a strategy to execute that strategy then accurately. Analyzing charts based on the strategy will allow for consistency in trading.

Questions to ask before choosing a technical analysis chart type:

- What is the trading strategy being adopted?
- Is the trading strategy targeting short, medium or long-term trades?

Once the above questions can be answered, the chart type may be chosen to utilize the individual information.

LEARN MORE ON TECHNICAL ANALYSIS

- Technical traders have different styles and strategies. Investigate these ultimately to see whether this sort of analysis suits your personality.
- We have a thorough introduction to technical analysis, which will help you structure a solid technical foundation.
- Supplement your understanding of technical analysis charts with our forex candlesticks article.
- Learn more about less popular charts like Heikin Ashi, Renko, and Point and Figure charts.

Practice Trading

It's currently an ideal opportunity to consider going all-in without surrendering your exchanging stake. Paper exchanging, or virtual exchanging, offers a perfect arrangement, permitting the novice to follow continuous market activities, settling on purchasing and selling choices that structure the blueprint of a hypothetical exhibition record. It generally includes utilizing a financial exchange test system to look and feel an actual stock trade's presentation. Do loads of businesses, using diverse holding periods and methodologies, and afterwards break down the outcomes for apparent imperfections.

Investopedia has a free securities exchange game, and numerous specialists let customers participate in paper exchanging with their genuine cash section frameworks. This has the additional advantage of instructing the product so you don't hit some unacceptable catches when playing with family reserves.

All in all, when do you do the switch and begin exchanging with genuine cash? There's no ideal answer because reproduced exchanging conveys a defect that will probably show up at whatever point you begin to trade seriously, regardless of whether your paper results look great.

Traders need to exist together calmly with the twin feelings of avarice and dread. Paper exchanging doesn't connect with these feelings, which must be capable by genuine benefit and misfortune. Indeed, this mental angle powers all the more first-year players out of the game than awful dynamic. Your child ventures forward as another trader needs to perceive this test and address remaining issues with cash and self-esteem.

While experience is a fine instructor, remember about extra training as you continue on your exchanging profession. Regardless of whether on the web or face to face, classes can be gainful, and you can discover them at levels going from amateur (with guidance on the best way to break down the previously mentioned scientific outlines, for instance) to genius. More particular courses—frequently led by an expert trader—can give essential knowledge into the general market and explicit speculation methodologies. Most spotlight on a specific resource, a particular part of the market, or an exchanging strategy. Some might be educational, and others more like workshops in which you effectively take positions, try out section and leave methodologies, and different activities (frequently with a test system).

Paying for examination and investigation can be both instructive and valuable. A few financial backers may discover watching or noticing market experts to be more beneficial than attempting to apply recently educated exercises themselves. There are many paid membership locales accessible across the web: Two all around regarded administrations incorporate Investors.com and Morningstar.

It's likewise helpful to get yourself a tutor—an involved mentor to manage you, study your procedure, and offer exhortation. On the off chance that you don't have any acquaintance with one, you can get one. Numerous web-based exchanging schools offer tutoring as a feature of their proceeding with ed programs.

Does practice make awesome? Indeed, we don't expect to be significant; however, we would like to be beneficial. Also, one approach to seeking after that objective is to practice, practice, practice on the paperMoney securities exchange test system on the thinkorswim exchanging stage.

paperMoney offers a virtual exchanging experience that allows you to test your exchanging procedures similarly as you would in a genuine, live circumstance yet without gambling a penny on an actual stock trade. A stock exchanging test system is an incredible route for anybody to sharpen their exchanging abilities, particularly if you:

- We need to have a go at exchanging stocks that don't yet have sufficient assets
- Have the money to trade yet aren't sure where to start
- Are an accomplished veteran trader yet need to utilize virtual exchanging to test new systems

In the first place, Install thinkorswim

Sign for to you at tdameritrade.com.

Go to the Trade tab. At the extreme right, select Start swimming today.

Select the green Download thinkorswim to fasten and introduce the stage.

When dispatching thinkorswim, slide the flip switch under your username and secret word to paperMoney before signing in (see figure 1).

You currently have virtual exchanging admittance to the more significant part of a similar set-up of instruments, outlines, and markers offered on the best in class thinkorswim live stage.

Be the Kid in the Candy Store

Since you're utilizing paperMoney, there could be no greater method to investigate the influence of the thinkorswim stage—with no danger—than by diving in and attempting a few things that you regularly wouldn't.

You can trade stocks in the exchanging test system. However, you can likewise do inside and out research on those biotech or fintech stocks you continue to find out about. Or then again, perhaps venture outside your usual range of familiarity and trade some new items or distinctive resource classes.

Is it accurate to say that you are a stock trader who's thinking about adding alternatives to your procedure? paperMoney permits you to try things out of fundamental choices techniques. Or, on the other hand, possibly you're keen on fates and forex markets, which exceptional retail traders and institutional financial backers use to conjecture and fence hazard. You may understand you appreciate approaching these items. Or then again, you may understand why such subordinate things aren't for everybody. (Note that not all financial backers will meet all requirements for choices, fates, or forex exchanging.)

paperMoney additionally offers you an incredible opportunity to evaluate distinctive graph pointers and studies to perceive how they work related to your exchange.

Instructions to Make the Most of Virtual Trading

Next, it's an ideal opportunity to foster your exchanging fortitude by zeroing in on the resources and procedures you're generally alright with. Here are five valuable hints to capitalize on the paperMoney securities exchange test system:

1. Upgrade your design. The paperMoney stage can be arranged and altered. For instance, the left segment gives "contraptions" for watch records, live news, Level II statements, Trader TV, and considerably more. There's even a scratch cushion to record trade notes. In principle screen, you can set up numerous diagrams in an adaptable matrix framework. Set aside a little effort to make the format that turns out best for you.

2. Utilize the force of information. Your exchanging information and history can be a fantastic learning instrument, and with paperMoney, it's all naturally readily available. paperMoney records every one of your trades (counting paper commissions) and gives a benefit and misfortune (P&L) investigation. Investigating this information routinely is a decent method to spot openings in your exchanging systems and fix them.

3. Trade "as though." When no cash is in danger, you can't get injured— however you should trade as though you can. If you trade outsize positions and face wild challenges, it will not assist you when it's an ideal opportunity to change to live to exchange. The influence of the virtual stock exchange enables you to refine a system expected for exchanging with genuine cash, so trade as though you are.

4. Utilize your "second chances." You will commit errors; that is the idea of learning and the explanation you're rehearsing. Yet, on the off chance that you think you've gone excessively far, don't be reluctant to begin once again without any preparation. You can do this by going to the Monitor tab on the upper left corner of the principle screen, looking down to the Position Statement line, and looking to the extreme right side. There you'll see a catch named Adjust Account. When chosen, you'll see an Account Adjustments box. Select Reset All Balances and Positions and hit Apply, and you'll get a fresh start (see figure 2).

5. Go on about your business. The more significant part of us doesn't have the advantage of sitting at an exchanging work area the entire day. Life interrupts, and we regularly must be somewhere else during the exchanging day. Be that as it may, actually like the live thinkorswim stage, the paperMoney financial exchange test system goes with you any place you go using the TD Ameritrade Mobile Trader application. Use it to practice overseeing trades in a hurry, similarly as you would with live exchanging.

Involved Learning
Need to practice exchanging reasonable market conditions without taking a chance with any genuine cash? Watch this stock exchanging test system instructional exercise to figure out how to utilize thinkorswim paperMoney and spot mimicked stock trades.

Chapter 3: Type of trading and difference between investing
An Introduction to Trading Types
Fundamental trading is a technique where a trader centres around organization explicit occasions to figure out which stock to purchase and when to get it. Trading on fundamentals is all the more firmly connected with

a purchase and-hold system instead of momentary trading. There are, nonetheless, explicit occurrences where trading on fundamentals can create significant benefits in a brief period.

Different Types of Traders

Before we centre around fundamental trading, here's a survey of the primary types of value trading:

Scalping: A hawker is a person who makes handfuls or many trades each day, trying to "scalp" a little benefit from each trade by misusing the bid-ask spread.

Force Trading: Momentum traders look for stocks that are moving essentially one way in high volume. These traders endeavour to ride the energy to the ideal benefit.

Specialized Trading: Technical traders centre around diagrams and charts. They break down lines on stock or list charts for indications of combination or dissimilarity that may show purchase or sell signals.

Fundamental Trading: Fundamentalists trade organizations dependent on the entire investigation, which analyzes corporate occasions, incredibly genuine or expected income reports, stock parts, redesigns, or acquisitions.

Swing Trading: Swing traders are fundamental traders who stand firm on their footings longer than a solitary day. Most fundamentalists are indeed swing trading since changes in corporate fundamentals typically require a few days or even a long time to deliver a value development adequate for the trader to guarantee a practical benefit.

Fledgeling traders may explore different avenues regarding every one of these procedures. Yet, they ought to eventually choose a solitary speciality coordinating with their contributing knowledge and involvement in a style to which they are roused to commit further examination, training, and practice.

Fundamental Data and Trading

Most value financial backers know about the most well-known financial information utilized in the fundamental investigation, including income per share (EPS), income, and income. These quantitative variables incorporate any figures found on an organization's income report, income articulation, or financial record. They can likewise include the consequences of economic proportions like profit from value (ROE) and obligation to value (D/E). Fundamental traders may utilize such quantitative information to recognize trading openings if, for instance, an organization issues income results that get the market unsuspecting.

Two of the most firmly watched fundamental components for traders and financial backers are profit declarations and investigator redesigns and downsize. Acquiring an edge on such data, notwithstanding, is troublesome since there are, in a real sense, a great many eyes on Wall Street searching for that same benefit.

Profit Announcements

The central part of income declarations is the pre-declaration stage—when an organization gives an assertion expressing whether it will meet, surpass or neglect to meet profit assumptions. Trades frequently happen following such a declaration because a momentary force opportunity will probably be accessible.

Examiner Upgrades and Downgrades

Additionally, investigator updates and downsizes may introduce a momentary trading opportunity, significantly when a noticeable expert surprisingly minimize a stock. The value activity in the present circumstance can be like a stone dropping from a bluff, so the trader should be speedy and deft with their short selling.

Profit declarations and examiner evaluations are likewise firmly connected with energy trading. Energy traders search for sudden occasions that cause a stock to trade an enormous volume of offers and move consistently either up or down.

The fundamental trader is frequently more worried about getting data on speculative occasions that the remainder of the market may need. To remain one stride in front of the market, sharp traders can regularly utilize their knowledge of verifiable trading designs that happen during the approach of stock parts, acquisitions, takeovers, and rearrangements.

Stock Splits

When a $20 stock parts 2-for-1, the organization's market capitalization doesn't change; however, the organization currently has twofold the number of remarkable offers at a $10 stock cost. Numerous financial backers accept that since financial backers will be more disposed to buy a $10 stock than a $20 stock, a stock split forecasts an expansion in the organization's market capitalization. In any case, recollect that this fundamentally doesn't change the worth of the organization.

To trade stock parts effectively, a trader must, most importantly, accurately recognize the stage at which the stock is at present trading. History has demonstrated that various explicit trading designs happen when a split declaration. Value appreciation and, subsequently, momentary purchasing openings will, for the most part, occur in the pre-declaration stage, and the pre-separated run and value devaluation (shorting gaps) will happen in the post-declaration sadness and post-split discouragement. By recognizing these four stages accurately, a split trader can trade all through similar stock at any rate on four separate occasions when the split with maybe a lot more intraday or even hour-by-hour trades.

Acquisitions, Takeovers, and More

The familiar aphorism "purchase the talk, sell the news" applies to those trading in acquisitions, takeovers, and rearrangements. In these cases, a stock will frequently encounter outrageous cost expansions in the theory stage, paving the way to the occasion, and huge decays following the event are declared.

The old financial backer's proverb "sell the information" should be qualified essentially for the insightful trader. A trader's down is to be out in front of the market. Accordingly, the trader will probably not purchase stock in a theoretical stage and hold it right to the genuine declaration. The trader is worried about catching a portion of the momenta in the speculative stage and may trade through similar stock a few times as the rumourmongers go to work. The trader may stand firm on a long foothold toward the beginning of the day and short in the early evening time being ever vigilant of outlines and Level 2 information for indications of when to change position.

When the actual declaration is made, the trader will probably have the chance to short the load of the procuring organization following it issues information on its plan to obtain, in this manner finishing the theoretical rapture paving the way to the declaration. Once in a while is an obtaining declaration seen decidedly, so shorting an organization that is doing the gaining is a stable twofold methodology.

Paradoxically, a corporate rearrangement will probably be seen absolutely on the off chance that the market did not expect it and if the stock had effectively been on a drawn-out slide because of inside corporate difficulties. On the off chance that a governing body out of nowhere expels a disliked CEO, for instance, a stock may show momentary vertical development in the news festival.

Trading the load of a takeover target is an exceptional case since a takeover offer will have a related cost for every request. A trader ought to be mindful of abstaining from stalling out holding stock at or close to the offer cost since offers will commonly not move altogether in the present moment once they track down their limited reach close to the objective. Mainly on account of a supposed takeover, the best trading openings will be in the theoretical stage (or the period when a reputed cost for each offer for the takeover offer will drive genuine value development).

Gossip and theory are dangerous trading recommendations, mainly on account of acquisitions, takeovers, and rearrangements. These occasions make outrageous stock-value instability. Be that as it may, due to the potential for fast value developments, these occasions likewise possibly fill in as the most rewarding fundamental trading openings accessible.

Mutual Fund over a Stock

Investing can be confounded and overpowering. There are countless different alternatives out there, from stocks and securities to land and currency market accounts. Whatever you pick, there's no assurance that you'll bring in cash from your speculations. However, there is an approach to make the most of the chances accessible in the market by pooling your money into one vehicle: A shared asset. You can positively assemble abundance by investing in stocks, yet it very well might be more secure to put resources into a shared asset, all things being equal. So for what reason would it be advisable for you to pick placing your cash into shared assets over stocks genuinely? Peruse on to discover probably the most well-known benefits that accompany investing in transferred assets.

The Basics of Mutual Funds

Shared assets pool cash all together of financial backers and put that capital into different protections like stocks, securities, currency market records, and others. Assets have various venture destinations to which their portfolios are customized. Cash supervisors are liable for each purchase. They produce to pay for financial backers by distributing resources inside the asset.

Shared assets can hold a wide range of protections, which makes them alluring venture alternatives. Among the reasons why an individual may decide to purchase shared assets rather than singular stocks are broadening, accommodation, and lower costs.

Scalping trading

Scalping is the most momentary type of trading. Scalp traders stand firm on footholds open for quite a long time or minutes. These fleeting trades target minor intraday value developments. The reason for existing is to make bunches of speedy trades with more modest benefit gains, yet let benefits collect for the day because of the sheer number of trades being executed in each trading meeting.

This way of trading requires tight spreads and fluid markets. Accordingly, hawkers will, in general, trade significant cash combines (because of liquidity and high trading volume), like EURUSD, GBPUSD, and USDJPY.

They likewise will, in general, the trade simply the busiest occasions of the trading day, during the cover of trading meetings when there is trading volume, and regularly instability. Hawkers search for the most impenetrable spreads conceivable, basically because they enter the market so habitually, so paying a more extensive spread will eat into possible benefits.

The quick-moving trading climate of attempting to scalp a couple of pips, whatever number occasions as could be allowed all through the trading day, can be distressing for some traders and is immensely tedious. Given the reality, you should zero in on outlines for a few hours all at once. As scalping can be extreme, hawkers will, in general, trade a couple of sets.

Scalping is the term utilized for the trading style with the briefest trading cycle—considerably more limited than different types of day trading. It got its name since traders who receive the kind—known as hawkers—rapidly enter and leave the market to skim little benefits off an enormous number of trades all through a trading day. They will likely make enough of these minor trades to amount to the help they might have produced using one-day trade with a higher benefit.

How Does Scalping Work?

Hawkers accept that it's safer to benefit from minor moves in stock costs than facing the challenge of enormous value moves. This includes setting tight trading windows, both as far as value development and period.

Scalping accompanies the lost chance expense of more significant increases, so it requires discipline. Hawkers escape trades once their benefit target has been hit, as opposed to holding on to check whether they can procure more. They likewise leave trades when their objective misfortune level has been shot instead of holding back to check whether the trade pivots.

Market Analysis for Scalping

Traders who receive this trading style depend on specialized examination rather than crucial investigation. Specialized examination is an approach to evaluate a stock's previous value development. Traders use graphs and markers to discover trading occasions and make section and leave focuses.

With the day's trading costs open continuously, diagrams, hawkers can notice a stock's value activity. Utilizing markers and known examples, they attempt to anticipate how a price will move in the following couple of moments or minutes. At that point, they set up low and high trading focuses and uses them to enter and leave trades.

Interestingly, the essential examination includes utilizing information from an organization's budget summaries. From the assertions, investors ascertain proportions that assist them with surveying an organization's worth dependent on their investment objectives. This permits them to evaluate an organization and oversee risks for developing their abundance after some time.

Hawkers may trade on news or occasions that adjust an organization's worth upon its delivery. At times, they may utilize momentary changes in central proportions to scalp trades. Generally, they center around specialized markers and outlines.

Since these diagrams demonstrate costs of the past, they lose esteem if the time skyline increments. The time skyline is how long a position is held. The more extended a hawker stands firm on a situation, the less worth that position will, in general, have for them. This is the reason specialized examination and trading pointers turn out better for the short idea of scalping.

Hawkers can be either optional or efficient traders. Optional hawkers rapidly settle on each trading choice dependent on market conditions. It is dependent upon the trader to choose the boundaries of each trade (timing, benefit targets, and so forth)

Methodical hawkers depend minimal on their impulses. All things being equal, they use PC programs that mechanize scalping. The projects utilize artificial brainpower to lead trades dependent on the measures set by the client. Whenever the program sees a trading opportunity, it acts without trusting that the trader will survey that position or trade.

Optional scalping brings predisposition into the trading interaction that can represent a danger. Feelings may entice you to make a terrible trade or neglect to make a move at a suitable time. Precise scalping removes human control from trading choices, making the trades fair.

Four simple scalping trading strategies

Scalp trading utilizing the stochastic oscillator

Scalping can be cultivated utilizing a stochastic oscillator. The term stochastic identifies with the mark of the current cost corresponding to its reach throughout a new timeframe. By contrast, the cost of security with its unique reach, a stochastic endeavors to give potential defining moments.

Scalping with the utilization of such an oscillator intends to catch moves in the moving market, i.e., one that is going up or down in a steady design.

In the above outline of Brent on a three-moment time, we can see that the cost is moving higher, and the lows in the stochastics (set apart with bolts) give section focuses too long trades when the dark %K line crosses over the specked red %D line. The trade is left when the stochastic arrives at the top finish of its reach, over 80, or when the bearish hybrid shows up when the %K line crosses underneath %D.

Conversely, short positions would be utilized in a descending moving market, with a model underneath. This time, rather than 'purchasing the plunges,' we are 'selling the assemblies.'

Scalp trading utilizing the moving normal

Another strategy is to utilize moving midpoints, generally with two moderately transient ones and any longer ones, to demonstrate the pattern.

In the models beneath, on a three-moment EUR/USD outline, we utilize five and 20-period moving midpoints (MA) for the present moment and a 200-period MA for the more drawn-out term. In the primary outline, the more drawn-out MA is rising, so we search for the five-time MA to cross over the 20 periods and afterward take positions toward the pattern. These are set apart with a bolt. The drawn-out MA is declining in the subsequent model, so we search for short positions when the value crosses underneath the five-time frame MA, which has effectively crossed beneath the 20-time frame MA. Recollect that these trades go with the pattern and that we are not hoping to get each move. As in all scalping, the board's right danger is fundamental, with stops indispensable to stay away from more considerable misfortunes that rapidly delete numerous little champs.

Scalp trading utilizing the explanatory SAR marker

The illustrative SAR is a pointer that features the bearing where a market moves and endeavors to give section and leave focuses. SAR means 'stop and inversion'. The information is a progression of specks put above or underneath the value bars. A spot underneath the cost is bullish, and one above is bearish.

An adjustment of the situation of the specks proposes that an adjustment of the pattern is in progress.

The outline underneath shows the DAX on a brief diagram; short trades can be taken when the value moves beneath the SAR specks and aches when the cost is above them. As can be seen, a few patterns are significantly expanded, and on different occasions, a trader will confront heaps of losing trades.

Scalp trading utilizing the RSI

At long last, traders can utilize the RSI to discover section focuses that go with the overarching pattern. The cost is moving consistently higher in the primary model, with the three moving midpoints extensively pointing higher.

Plunges in the pattern are to be purchased, so when the RSI drops to 30 and afterward moves over this line, a potential passage point is made.

What you need to know before scalping

Scalping requires a trader to have an iron order, yet it is also highly requesting time. While longer-term and more modest sizes permit traders to move back from their foundation, since potential sections are more minor and can be observed in a good way, scalping requests a trader's complete consideration.

Conceivable section focuses can show up and vanish rapidly, and in this manner, a trader should stay attached to his foundation. For people with day occupations and different exercises, scalping isn't an ideal technique. Longer-term trades with more excellent benefit targets are more fit.

Scalping is a troublesome procedure to execute effectively. One of the fundamental reasons is that it requires numerous trades over time. Examination regarding this matter will, in general, show that more continuous traders lose cash all the more rapidly and have a negative value bend. All things being equal, most traders would discover more achievement, and diminish their time responsibilities to trading, and surprisingly cut down on pressure by searching for long haul trades and try not to scalp procedures.

Scalping requires speedy reactions to market developments and a capacity to swear off a trade if the specific second is missed. 'Pursuing' trades, alongside an absence of stop misfortune discipline, are the key reasons that hawkers are regularly fruitless. The possibility of just being in the market for a brief timeframe sounds appealing; however, the odds of being halted on an unexpected move that rapidly turns around are high.

Trading is a movement that prizes persistence and control. While those fruitful in scalping do show these characteristics, they are a modest number. Most traders are in an ideal situation with a more extended term see, more modest position sizes, and a less exciting speed of action.

Day trading

For those that are not happy with the power of scalp trading, yet at the same time don't wish to stand firm on footholds short-term, day trading may suit.

Informal investors enter and leave their situations around the same time (not at all like swing and position traders), eliminating the danger of any huge overnight moves. By the day's end, they close their situation with either a benefit or a misfortune. Trades are generally held for minutes or hours and subsequently require an adequate chance to dissect the markets and regularly screen positions for the day. Very much like scalp traders, informal investors depend on regular little gains to assemble benefits.

Informal investors give incredibly close consideration to key and specialized examination, utilizing technical pointers like MACD, the Relative Strength Index, and the Stochastic Oscillator to help distinguish patterns and market conditions.

Day trading is the demonstration of purchasing and selling a monetary instrument around the same time or even on various occasions throughout the day. Exploiting minor value moves can be a worthwhile game—on the off chance that it is played accurately. In any case, it tends to be a dangerous game for beginners or any individual who doesn't stick to a thoroughly examined methodology.

Not all agents are appropriate for the high volume of trades made by informal investors, in any case. Be that as it may, a few intermediaries are planned, given the everyday investor. You can look at our rundown of the best merchants for day trading to see which intermediaries best oblige the individuals who might want to day trade.

The online merchants on our rundown, Fidelity and Interactive Brokers, have proficient or progressed variants of their foundation that element continuous streaming statements, progressed diagramming devices, and the capacity to enter and alter complex orders one after another.

Beneath, we'll investigate some broad day trading standards and afterward proceed onward to choosing when to purchase and sell, regular day trading methodologies, essential graphs, and examples, and how to restrict misfortunes.

1. Information Is Power

Notwithstanding information on fundamental trading strategies, informal investors need to keep up on the most recent stock market news and occasions that influence stocks—the Fed's loan cost designs, the monetary viewpoint, and so forth.

So get your work done. Make a list of things to get of stocks you'd prefer to trade and keep yourself educated about the chose organizations and general markets. Sweep business news and visit solid monetary sites.

2. Put Away Funds

Survey how much capital you're willing to risk on each trade. Numerous fruitful informal investors assume under 1% to 2% of their record per trade. If you have a $40,000 trading account and will change 0.5% of your capital on each trade, your greatest misfortune per trade is $200 (0.5% * $40,000).

Put away an excess measure of assets you can trade with, and you're set up to lose. Keep in mind, and it could occur.

3. Put Away Time, Too

Day trading requires your time. That is the reason it's called day trading. You'll have to surrender a large portion of your day. Try not to consider it if you have restricted extra time.

The cycle requires a trader to follow the markets and spot openings, which can emerge whenever trading hours. Rushing is critical.

4. Start Small

As an amateur, center around a limit of one to two stocks during a meeting. Following and discovering openings is more straightforward with only a couple stocks. As of late, it has gotten progressively typical to have the option to trade fragmentary offers, so you can determine explicit, more modest dollar sums you wish to invest.

That implies if Apple shares are trading at $250 and you need to purchase $50 worth, numerous representatives will currently allow you to buy one-fifth of an offer.

5. Keep away from Penny Stocks

You're likely searching at arrangements and low costs; however, avoid penny stocks. These stocks are frequently illiquid, and the odds of hitting a significant stake are regularly disheartening.

Numerous stocks trading under $5 an offer become de-recorded from significant stock trades and are just tradable over-the-counter (OTC). Except if you see a genuine chance and have done your examination, avoid these.

6. Time Those Trades

Numerous orders put by investors and traders start to execute when the markets open toward the beginning of the day, which adds to value instability. A prepared player might have the option to perceive examples and pick suitably to make benefits. Yet, for novices, it very well might be better to peruse the market without taking any actions for the initial 15 to 20 minutes.

The center hours are typically less unstable, and afterward, development starts to get again toward the end chime. Even though the times of heavy traffic offer freedoms, it's more secure for amateurs to stay away from them from the start.

7. Cut Losses With Limit Orders

Choose what sort of requests you'll use to enter and leave trades. Will you utilize market requests or breaking point orders? When you submit a market request, it's executed at the best cost accessible at that point—consequently, no value ensure.

A breaking point request, in the meantime, ensures the cost, however, not the execution. Breaking point orders help you trade with more accuracy, wherein you set your price (not ridiculous however executable) for purchasing just like selling. More complex and experienced informal investors may utilize the utilization of choices procedures to fence their situations too.

8. Be Realistic About Profits

A methodology doesn't have to win constantly to be productive. Numerous traders win half to 60% of their trades. Nonetheless, they make more on their champs than they lose on their failures. Ensure the danger on each trade is restricted to a particular level of the record and that passage and leave strategies are characterized and recorded.

9. Stay Cool

There are times when the stock markets test your nerves. As an informal investor, you need to figure out how to keep ravenousness, expectation, and dread under control. Choices ought to be administered by rationale and not feeling.

10. Stay on course

Fruitful traders need to move quickly, yet they don't need to think fast. Why? Since they've fostered a trading procedure ahead of time, alongside the order to adhere to that system. It is imperative to follow your equation intently instead of attempt to pursue benefits. Try not to allow your feelings to outwit you and surrender your technique. There's a mantra among informal investors: "Plan your trade and trade your arrangement."

Before we go into a portion of the intricate details of day trading, how about we take a gander at a part of the reasons why day trading can be so troublesome.

How Much Can You Make as a Day Trader?

What amount of cash does the average informal investor make? The inquiry is challenging to reply to. Hardly any casual investors uncover their outcomes to anybody yet the Internal Revenue Service. Additionally, results change generally given the bunch of trading techniques, risk the board practices, and capital accessible for day trading.

Undoubtedly, losing cash at day trading is simple. An examination paper from University of California scientists Brad Barber and Terrance Odean tracked down that numerous individual investors hold undiversified portfolios and trade effectively, theoretically, and their impairment.

Informal investors can likewise bring about high financier charges, so picking the best representative and making a sensible trading methodology with legitimate danger the executives is fundamental.

What Day Traders Do

Informal investors regularly target stocks, choices, prospects, items, or monetary standards, standing firm on footholds for quite a long time or minutes before selling once more. Informal investors enter and leave positions inside the day, subsequently the term casual investors. They once in a while stand firm on footings short-term. The objective is to benefit from momentary value developments. Informal investors can likewise utilize influence to enhance returns, which can again intensify misfortunes.

Setting stop-misfortune orders and benefit taking focuses—and not taking on an excess of risk—is essential to making due as an informal investor. Proficient traders regularly suggest taking a chance with close to 1% of your portfolio on a solitary trade. If a portfolio is valued at $50,000, the most in danger per trade is $500. The way to overseeing risks is not to permit a couple of awful trades to clear you out. Suppose you adhere to a 1% danger procedure and set strict stop-misfortune orders and benefit-taking focuses. In that case, you can restrict your misfortunes to 1% and take your benefits at 1.5%, yet it takes discipline.

The most effective method to Get Started in Day Trading

Beginning in day trading isn't care for fiddling with investing. Any future investor with a couple of hundred dollars can purchase portions of an organization and save it for quite a long time or years. Notwithstanding, the Financial Industry Regulatory Authority (FINRA) sets rules for those they characterize, for example, informal investors. These standards require edge traders who trade as often as possible to keep up, in any event, $25,000 in their records, and they can't trade if their equilibrium dips under that level.2 This implies informal investors should have adequate capital on top of the $25,000 to make a benefit truly. Furthermore, because day trading requires a center, it isn't viable to keep average everyday employment.

Most informal investors ought to be set up to chance their capital. Notwithstanding required equilibrium essentials, imminent casual investors need admittance to an online specialist or trading stage and programming to follow positions, do research, and log trades. Financier commissions and expenses on transient capital increases can likewise add up. Hopeful informal investors should consider all costs of their trading exercises to decide whether the benefit is feasible.

Procuring Potential and Career Longevity

A significant factor that can impact profit potential and professional life span is whether you day trade freely or for a foundation, for example, a bank or flexible investments. Traders working at an organization don't change their cash and are regularly promoted, with admittance to valuable data and instruments. In the meantime, some autonomous trading firms permit informal investors to get to their foundation and programming yet expect traders to risk their capital.

Other significant elements that affect an informal investor's profit potential include:

Markets you trade: Different markets enjoy various benefits. Stocks are by and large the most capital-escalated resource class. People can begin trading with less capital than with other resource classes, like prospects or forex.

How much capital you have: If you start with $3,000, your profit potential is undeniably short of somebody who begins with $30,000.

Time: Few informal investors make progress in only a couple of days or weeks. Beneficial trading procedures, frameworks, and approaches can require a very long time to create.

Trading choices is altogether different from trading stocks since alternatives have unmistakable qualities from stocks. Investors need to set aside the effort to comprehend the phrasing and ideas associated with choices prior to trading them.

Choices are monetary subordinates, implying that they get their worth from the fundamental security or stock. Alternatives give the purchaser the right, yet not the commitment, to purchase or sell the hidden stock at a pre-decided cost.

Conclusion

There is a ton of data stuffed into this book to attempt to assist you with being set up to trade stocks and, particularly, alternatives utilizing specialized investigation. Trading is an interaction, and like any cycle, the more pre-arranged you are and the more practice you get, the better you can be grinding away. I began this book with a statement from Seneca—"Karma is the thing that happens whenever planning meets opportunity"— and have composed the parts from that point of view. It would help if you were prepared to trade and be set up to exploit any karma that the market gives you. You presently know the stuff to be arranged, in any event, to trade from a specialized point of view.

The initial segment of the book, "Recognizing and Understanding the Trend," began the cycle. We investigated how to recognize the significant pattern and what impacts it in Chapter 1. This is significant because 70% or a greater amount of all stocks move with the pattern. We, at that point, investigated the areas in Chapter 2, one layer further into the onion of the market design to see where to centre. With simply these two cycles dominated, you are set up to settle on the greatest choices of your investing and trading life, addressing the inquiry "What direction is the market moving, and how would I utilize that data?" If you have gotten nothing else out of this book except for comprehension of how to distinguish the pattern and benefit by trading with it, at that point, I have prevailed in my undertaking. In any case, there was much more.

The end is never to trade without a genuinely demonstrated trading model. This last area rattles off the agenda for the trader to finish the last check before he starts trading effectively. He drafts his trading plan, including numerous markets. To track down the best trading instrument, explicit exploration information investigation on occasions arrangement and tests on the most beneficial ones are finished. The most reasonable specialized pointer, as flexible moving normal, is chosen, further developed and tried to make it work for him. He composes his formulae into his trading program, including the stop misfortune for hazard the executives. He deals with his capital well. Inspecting and occasional minds the trading diary keep the trading framework refreshed. Finishing the schedule, he begins trading.

Lightning Source UK Ltd.
Milton Keynes UK
UKHW020638100621
385271UK00011B/634